Victorian and Edwardian
OXFORDSHIRE

1   Vice-Chancellor T.H. Warren signals to the assembled
heads of University and City the end of the Edwardian era
with the proclamation of King George V, May 1910

2 The annual horse fair, held near Banbury's famous cross
for four days in January, attracted horses and dealers from
far and wide. The 'cross' was built in 1859 to commemorate
the marriage of Victoria, the Princess Royal, to the Crown
Prince of Prussia

Victorian and Edwardian

OXFORDSHIRE

from old photographs

Introduction and commentaries by

MARY CLAPINSON

B.T. BATSFORD LTD
LONDON

First published 1978
Copyright Mary Clapinson 1978

Filmset in 'Monophoto' Apollo by
Servis Filmsetting Ltd, Manchester
Printed in Great Britain by
The Anchor Press Ltd, Tiptree, Essex
for the publishers B.T. Batsford Ltd,
4 Fitzhardinge Street, London W1H 0AH

ISBN 0 7134 1059 0

3   Mr G. Budd delivering the bread in about 1900. His
family had been bakers in Woodstock from at least 1830

CONTENTS

Acknowledgments

Introduction

ACKNOWLEDGMENTS

I should like to thank David Vaisey, Keeper of Western Manuscripts at the Bodleian Library, for all his encouragement and help with this book; Mr Frederick Anker of Banbury, Shirley Barnes of Oxfordshire County Record Office, Christine Bloxham, Crispin Paine and John Rhodes of Oxfordshire County Council's Museum Services, David Brown of Oxfordshire Education Department, Miss G. H. Dannatt of Bicester, Mr Elsey of Thame, Malcolm Graham of Oxfordshire County Libraries, Mr E. J. Kahn of Bloxham School, Dr G. Lloyd Jones of Ripon College, Mr Ernest Pocock of Clanfield, Dora Rayson of Manchester Central Library, Elizabeth Reed of Shilton, Mrs G. Rosengarde of Broadwell, Mrs A. J. Simpson of Goring, and Ian Wilkinson of Fulbrook, for help in locating and identifying photographs; John Knight, Shirley Baker and especially Charles Braybrooke and the staff of the Bodleian Library photographic studio for copying the old photographs reproduced here.

For permission to reproduce the photographs indicated, I am indebted to: Oxfordshire County Libraries, nos. 5, 7–9, 12, 14, 16–17, 19–20, 25–6, 28, 33–4, 47, 52, 57, 63, 70–1, 76, 79, 85, 89, 92–3, 95–7, 102–5, 120, 125–6, 128, 133, 142 (all but nos. 52, 70, 120 by Henry Taunt); the Bodleian Library, nos. 1, 11, 13, 15, 36, 40, 48, 56, 61, 72, 83, 121–2, 127, 136; Banbury Museum, nos. 2, 4, 18, 35, 37, 39, 41, 62, 64, 74–5, 90, 106, 109–10, 138; Oxfordshire County Council Museum Services, nos. 24, 49, 51, 53–5, 58–60, 82, 87, 91, 101, 143; George Bushell and Son of Henley, nos. 29–31, 69, 78, 81, 86, 88, 129–32, 140–1, 145; Goring History Society, nos. 66–7, 98–100, 123–4; Packer's Studio of Chipping Norton, nos. 21–3, 77, 94, 147; Miss Florence Budd of Woodstock, nos. 3, 38, 73, 107, 139; Mr George Swinford of Filkins, nos. 44–6, 119, 137; Oxfordshire Education Department, nos. 114–18; Mr Fred Smith of Bucknell, nos. 32, 65, 108, 146; Bloxham School, nos. 111–13; Ripon College, Cuddesdon, nos. 134–5; Science Museum, London, nos. 6, 10; Miss Ivy Beckinsale of Langford, no. 42; Blinkhorns of Banbury, no. 144; Mrs J. M. L. Clack of Standlake, no. 55; Mr W. A. Clarke, Managing Director of Hook Norton Brewery Co., no. 68; Mr Edwin Eagle of Standlake, no. 53; Mr John Foreshaw of Kencot, no. 43; Mrs W. M. Fox of Weston on the Green, no. 87; Miss Jane Harris of Ascot, Berks., no. 54; Horspath Parish Council, no. 84; Mrs Hilda Hunt of Shilton, no. 50; Mr John Mawle of South Leigh, no. 59; Museum of English Rural Life, Reading, no. 80; Mrs S. Tarver of Burdrop, no. 58; Mrs Stella Taylor of Upper Tysoe, no. 60; David Vaisey, no. 27.

INTRODUCTION

4 Ices for sale at Banbury market, August 1897

For centuries Oxfordshire has had one centre of attraction for the visitor – the city and university of Oxford. Antiquaries and topographers in the seventeenth and eighteenth centuries, like many of the tourists of the present day for whom Oxford is the stopping point en route from London to Stratford, afforded the county only a cursory glance on their way to see the architectural beauties of the university and city. Oxford is, of course, (or was until the boundary changes of 1974) on the very edge of the county – a county which in the nineteenth century had no great spa to draw the fashionable world across its borders, no first class racecourse to act as a magnet for the sportsmen, and no coastline to attract the devotees of the new pastime of sea bathing. To be sure the owners of the great houses with which the county is liberally supplied held their house parties: the Dukes of Marlborough at Blenheim Palace, the Earls of Jersey at Villiers Park, the Viscounts Dillon at Ditchley, the Harcourts at Nuneham Courtenay, the Dashwoods at Kirtlington Park and the Brassey family at Heythrop; but there was nothing else outside Oxford itself which would hold for long the attention of the visitor. This is reflected in such early photographs as are known to survive (nos. 6, 10) of Oxford High Street and Tom Tower, Christ Church, both taken by the pioneer of photography, William Henry Fox Talbot, in about 1845. It is only with the popularization of the postcard at the turn of the century that one begins to find general views of places other than Oxford. Even then at least ten postcards of Oxford colleges and streets seem to have survived for every one of the county. Only a few photographs of Oxford life have been included in this book, as the events, buildings and people of the city and university have already been illustrated in an earlier volume in this series, by Sir John Betjeman and David Vaisey.

The countryside around Oxford is far from spectacular, indeed the 'Shell' guide to Oxfordshire describes it as 'one of the most ordinary of the English counties'. Its attractions in the Victorian age, as in the eighteenth century, were quietly rural, those of an area of fertile fields and meadows, gentle hills and rivers, about which few visitors would have waxed so eloquent as D. Jones in his *New Description of England and Wales* in 1724:

> It abounds with all sorts of game and is fruitful in grass and corn; but though it bears the last very well, yet its greatest glory is the abundance of meadows and pastures.

Most visitors, like the author of *England Delineated* in 1788 would reserve the title of the county's 'great glory' to 'its capital, the city of Oxford, containing the largest of the two English universities, a seat of learning, with the reputation of which the whole literary world is sufficiently acquainted'. The glories of the city of Oxford, its spectacular skyline, its historic buildings and beautiful streets, have long overshadowed its quiet surroundings. The Victorian photographer, anxious to interest and impress his public, naturally took pictures of the unique city and to a large extent ignored the ordinary countryside around it.

A remarkably detailed picture of life in Victorian Oxfordshire has survived in the work of Flora Thompson. *Lark Rise*, the first section of her now-famous trilogy, gives what is perhaps the best and most evocative picture of rural life in any English county at that time. A sensitive child, brought up in the hamlet of Juniper Hill in the north-east corner of Oxfordshire, she put into words the day to day life of the agricultural labourers, the rural craftsmen and their families in the 1880s and 1890s, with unrivalled clarity and understanding. The world she described, which came to an end when men like her brother marched off to war in 1914, is the world in which lived most of the people captured here by the camera; a world as yet, when the first photographs were taken, unshrunk by the motor car and the telegraph; a world in which for many the horizon was the parish boundary. The present selection brings together in one book a wide variety of photographs, from different parts of the county, and in so doing imposes a common world on them. It is as well to remember, though, that the differences in their customs and their ways of life were likely to have been as marked as the visible differences in the stone of their houses and the shape of their wagons (nos. 28, 82), or the audible difference in accent still noticeable between those who live in the north, the west and the south of the county. The children in *Lark Rise* could wonder whether heaven was farther away than Banbury, and knew nothing of Oxford beyond the reports of 'a gert big town' where wages (and rents) were high, and where the houses had no gardens for growing vegetables or for keeping a pig. The adult inhabitants of Juniper Hill would not necessarily have thought of themselves as living the same sort of lives as their contemporaries in the villages of Wardington and Sibford to the north, Filkins and Standlake in the west, or Iffley and Shiplake in the south. Still less would they have classed themselves with the townspeople of Banbury, Witney or Henley.

That any photographic record of Victorian Oxfordshire survives outside the family album is largely the result of the work of one local man – Henry Taunt of Oxford. Born in 1842, the son of a plumber and glazier, Taunt took a job with Edward Bracher, photographic artist in the High Street, in 1856. Two years later, he was taking photographs out of doors, leaving his employer to concentrate on the more fashionable and lucrative work in the studio. Before his death in 1922, Taunt built up his own business as a photographer and publisher, and left the enormous number of 60,000 negatives. He was also a keen amateur antiquarian, aware of the importance photographs could have in recording landscapes, buildings and customs which were changing rapidly or disappearing altogether. There were, of course, other commercial photographers at work in the county during this period, but most were, like Bracher, concentrating on taking portraits in their studios. None of them was in business for anything like Taunt's 54 years, and their work has not survived in bulk as Taunt's has. The local directories give an indication of the growth of commercial photography during these years. In 1864, 14 photographers are listed, of whom ten were in Oxford, two in Banbury, one in Burford and one in Deddington. By 1895, the city of Oxford alone had 21 photographers, Banbury had five, and Deddington still had one, though it was a different firm. Photographic businesses were much more widely spread over the county, with three in Henley, two each in Witney, Chipping Norton and Caversham, and one each in Bicester, Crowmarsh Gifford, Dorchester, Eynsham, Watlington and Woodstock. Of these towns and villages, Henley is fortunate to have a firm of photographers who have preserved the work of their predecessors, the beautiful photographs of the Market Place and Northfield End in the 1850s and 1860 (nos 29, 30) and of the frozen Thames in the winter of 1894–5 (nos 131–2). Similarly, Chipping Norton's present photographic studio, established in the first years of this century, has preserved much early work, here represented by the photographs of that town and its tradesmen (nos 21–3). Banbury's historian, William

Potts, made it his business to preserve many photographs which might otherwise have disappeared. Examples of these are the evocative pictures of Wardington church path, the Eaves family of Williamscot and the ices stall at Banbury market, reproduced here (nos 4, 39, 64) from his lantern slides.

Family albums and collections are another rich source of photographs for the period. Even those which might be considered to be only of family interest can become valuable evidence of a way of life which has disappeared. A fine example of this is the collection of the Simpson family of Goring. Mr and Mrs Arthur Telford Simpson moved into a large house on the banks of the Thames in the late 1890s. He was an eminent engineer and a magistrate, who, with his wife, took an active part in village and county affairs. Their photographs are tremendously evocative of the elegance and gracious living of the Edwardian era (nos 99, 100) and incidentally provide evidence of leisure activities (nos 123–4) and modes of transport (nos 66–7). Similarly the extensive collection of the Budd family of Woodstock provides illustrations of shops and trades in that town (nos 3, 38), a vanished railway (no. 73) and local musical and military events (nos 107, 139).

Greater social mobility, the metalled road, the motor car, the long distance coach, have brought more visitors into the county this century, attracted by the growth of industry and the European importance of Banbury's cattle market on the one hand, and by the transformation of the houses of the great landowners into 'stately homes' open to the public, Henley regatta, Thames river cruises, steam fairs, and the associations of the county with Sir Winston Churchill on the other. Such visitors, as well as those who know the county well, will instantly recognize many of the views in this section. The High Street of Woodstock (no. 17) and Burford (no. 19), Witney's Market Place (no. 25), and Church Street, Charlbury (no. 36) have retained their character and most of their buildings, though some houses, inevitably, have been altered or demolished. The photographs amply show, too, that great pride of the county – its building stone. The grey limestone of the west, principally quarried at Taynton, Swinbrook and Kit's Quarries, gives Burford and Woodstock (nos 19, 17) a delightful aspect and transforms otherwise ordinary buildings, like the barn near Shilton (no. 50) and Florey's farmhouse, Brighthampton (no. 55). The northern part of the county is dominated by the beautiful brown ironstone which was quarried at Hornton. Some idea of the richness of the stone is given even in black-and-white photographs, for example those of the cottage at Sibford (no. 58), Wardington church (no. 39) and Wroxton Abbey (no. 109). The beautiful Stonesfield slates of west Oxfordshire stand out clearly in the views of Witney and Burford High Streets (nos 24, 19). On the barn near Shilton (no. 50) they make an interesting contrast with the thatch on a similar building in Adderbury in the north of the county (no. 49). The locally made brick and tile so characteristic of the south and east is best illustrated in the very early example of the fifteenth-century almhouses at

Ewelme (no. 56). Milcombe, near Bloxham, already showed in 1910 some of the roofing material which was to become so prevalent in English villages – corrugated iron (no. 41).

Although many of the places are immediately recognizable to us from these pictures, we are a long way removed from the individuals who people those places, whose society Flora Thompson so vividly chronicled. The wealth of the large landowners was conspicuous; the great gulf between landed and landless is again and again shown by the photographs, and through them all, the enormous importance of agriculture is apparent. The main function of the country towns was still the holding of markets, an outlet for the produce of the surrounding area; either on a domestic level, like the country-woman with her stall at Banbury market (no. 35), or on a large scale like the livestock markets of Thame, Bicester and Chipping Norton (nos 28, 32, 22), which bring life to the street scenes. Even as late as 1911 over 25% of men in the county were farm labourers, though their rates of pay were lower here than almost anywhere else in the country. In 1907 Beatrice A. Lees (in the Victoria County History) could still write of rural villages sleeping on 'undisturbed in their peaceful seclusion' and of a country of 'archaic survivals and old world traditions' only a few miles from the bustling centre of Oxford. Two such survivals are illustrated in the May Day celebrations at Iffley (no. 57) and the Bampton Morris Men (no. 105). It was in this county, at Headington, that Cecil Sharp in 1899 made his first study of the tunes of Morris dances, which was to bear fruit in the English Folk-Dance Society.

The principal industries of Victorian and Edwardian Oxfordshire were those which depended on the products of agriculture or catered for its needs. All the towns and most of the villages had their craftsmen – blacksmiths, carpenters, wheelwrights and saddlers – who were geared to serving the agricultural community. Many of the blacksmiths turned their hand to making farm implements; John Moss of Henley (no. 81) was typical of many small firms of agricultural machine makers all over the county. On a larger scale, Bernard Samuelson's works in Banbury produced agricultural implements which were sold throughout England. Men like Edwin Gardner and his son Harry served the rural community around Shilton in a way which has no equivalent today. They set up their cider press in villages of the area, and people could bring their own apples to be pulped in it (no. 90).

The fine wool and rivers of the Cotswold region provided the raw material and favourable conditions for the manufacture of blankets at Witney (nos 92–3) and tweed at Chipping Norton. Both these industries have survived to the present day. Indeed, the former adapted so successfully to the machine age that Witney blankets are now the best known of all the county's manufactures. That the transition into modern times was not always a smooth one is illustrated in the photograph of Bliss's tweed mill, guarded by policemen in 1913–14 (no. 94). The firm, founded in 1757, was proud of its reputation as a good employer, which had never had disputes with its workforce. The Workers' Union, aiming to organize workers employed in rural areas and small towns, began to recruit members in Chipping Norton and Witney. Three of its members were dismissed from Bliss's mill and the other unionists went on strike in support of their colleagues. Lack of funds brought the strike to an end in May 1914, with none of its objectives achieved. Earlier efforts to establish a trade union to protect the interests of farm labourers had failed in the previous century. The demand for wages higher than the basic weekly rate of 11 or 12 shillings had at first been successful in the county in 1871 and 1872, but the slump in agricultural prices had gradually weakened the labourers' bargaining power, and by 1892 no branch of the Agricultural Labourers' Union existed in Oxfordshire.

Many of the industries which employed large numbers of people in Oxfordshire in the nineteenth century have not survived into the present. Burford and Bampton were centres for the production of saddles and leather goods. Withies were cultivated along many rivers (no. 85), and basket makers, such as Watts at Chipping Norton (no. 23), flourished in most towns. Cottage industries like lace-making in the Chilterns and plush-weaving around Banbury (no. 91) succumbed to competition from factories in the Midlands. The making of Stonesfield slates, in the village of that name to the west of Woodstock, came to an end in 1909, using to the last the winter frosts to split the mined blocks of pendle into the slates needed for roofing. Other industries, like glove-making around Woodstock and brewing at Hook Norton (no. 68) and Henley (no. 81), have survived on a modest scale.

One of the main causes of the changes in society in Oxfordshire which make the people of these photographs seem so far-removed from us, was the introduction of new means of transport. This is well-illustrated in the photographs themselves. The number of horses and carriages of one sort and another that appear in the street scenes (e.g. nos 26, 31) provides ample evidence of the key role of the wheelwright and saddler in Victorian society. The increasing use of and interest in traction and diesel engines is seen in the number of times they are photographed in the 1890s and the first years of the twentieth century (nos 68–70). Advertisements for petrol beside the sheep market at Chipping Norton (no. 22) and the horse fair at Bampton (no. 34) are a clear indication of change on the way. The advent of the motor car, to which Oxford contributed so much through W.R. Morris, was to change the towns, villages and countryside more drastically than anything in the past.

The railways, still expanding in Oxfordshire in 1908 (no. 83), had already left their mark during this period. The Great Western and the London and North-Western Railways vied with each other to connect Banbury by rail with London and the Midlands. They both opened stations there in 1850 and the improvement in communications greatly enhanced the importance of Banbury's market, and encouraged the development of industries on a larger scale. By contrast, Burford, which in its heyday had 40 stage coaches stopping in its High Street each day, was by-passed, first by the top road (now the A40) and then by the railway. Its only link with the railway network was a service of horse buses, run by Thomas Paintin to Shipton station five miles away (no. 63). As a result Burford found its market dwindling in importance. No industries survived or established themselves in the town in the nineteenth century (except the small brewery of the Garne family), and Burford became fossilized as a small country town, much admired by tourists and by students of urban architecture.

Any collection of Victorian and Edwardian photographs is valuable as a record of the buildings, landscapes and events of a past age. Their ability to reproduce things as they really were makes them an extremely useful source of information for the historian on both the local and the national level. It is clearly important to be able to study, for example, the streets of the country towns before the invasion of the motor car and lorry, a horse-drawn tram in Oxford or a horse bus in Burford, the interior of a blanket mill at Witney or of a printing works in Oxford, and the structure of the windmill at Charlton on Otmoor which was demolished in 1905. These photographs provide a record of such things which is often more informative than any other surviving source; but their real interest lies for most of us in the insight they give into a way of life so different from our own. Against a background of the countryside, villages and towns of Oxfordshire, which is in many ways familiar to us, the photographs capture people and a society which have disappeared for ever. The pictures which hold the attention longest are those of groups of people at work in the fields and factories, and at play on the river or at the fair; of children in the classrooms of village schools at the beginning of Edward VII's reign; unknown individuals like the two oldest people in Sibford at the turn of the century and the blacksmith at Bampton in 1904, or eminent Victorians like Bishop Samuel Wilberforce and William Morris. Distant though the days of Queen Victoria's reign are, the way of life of her subjects is revealed to us, with clarity and insight, through a medium not available for any earlier age – the photograph.

OXFORD –
TOWN & GOWN

5   Town watches gown: the procession to Encaenia leaving
Vice-Chancellor Magrath's college, Queen's, headed by the
Chief Constable, Oswald Cole, 1897

6 *Left* Oxford High Street, taken by W.H. Fox Talbot, the pioneer of photography, in about 1845. The buildings on the right, beyond the elaborate porch of St Mary's Church, were demolished in 1886 to make way for Brasenose College's New Building

8 *Below* The cattle market at Gloucester Green in about 1885. The market moved to the Oxpens site in 1931. The row of old buildings on the right was replaced by a school in 1900

7 *Left* The west end of the High Street in 1887, with a horse tram travelling east. All but the tower of the city church at Carfax was demolished in 1896 for road-widening

11 *Right* The week after the end of Trinity Term, Commemoration Week, was the occasion for many social celebrations in the University. This fashionable group attended the Encaenia Luncheon at Magdalen College on 22 June 1898. A.E. Cowley, orientalist and (from 1919) Bodley's Librarian is second from the left in the back row

9 Broad Street in about 1887, before the Indian Institute building dominated the east end

10 *Below right* Oxford's most famous tower, Tom Tower of Christ Church, photographed by Fox Talbot in about 1845. The statue of Cardinal Wolsey, which now occupies the niche in the window above the arch, though made in 1719, was not put there until 1872. The quadrangle is not yet adorned by Mercury, the most photographed statue in Oxford

12 *Above* The Queen's College barge packed with sightseers
during Eights Week, 1890

13 *Below* Magdalen College crew at the starting point,
Eights Week, May 1892

14 Less formal boating, on the River Cherwell, north of the University Parks, in about 1895

15 *Above* Nuneham Courtenay was a favourite spot for picnics, within easy boating reach of the University. The distinguished company here, on 28 June 1890, includes (in the back row) the orientalist, A.E. Cowley on the left, the classical scholar, A.D. Godley in the middle, and H.W. Greene, later vice-principal of Magdalen

16 *Below* An undergraduate's room, *c.*1895. The popularity of the new art of portrait photography is demonstrated by the contents of every shelf and small table

THE COUNTRY TOWNS

17 The High Street, Woodstock, in the 1890s. The shop of
Budd the baker (see no. 3) is the second on the left

18 *Left* Market day in Banbury High Street, 1898. Cattle continued to be sold in the streets until the increase in motor traffic necessitated the construction of a covered market in the Grimsbury area of the town in 1925

19 *Right* The fair in Burford High Street in about 1900. Traditionally the Michaelmas fair had been a festive occasion, with the main business the sale of cheeses and toys and the hiring of servants. After a gradual decline, the practice of hiring carters, labourers and general servants came to an end in 1914

20 *Below* The sixteenth-century Tolsey in Burford, in the 1890s. Originally a market house, it had by then become the fire station on the ground floor, and a reading room above. The building at the rear had been used as a lock-up until the establishment of the County Police in the 1860s

21 *Above* The shop of Edwin Minchin in the Market Place, Chipping Norton, in about 1905. The coming of motorized transport tolled the death-knell of such important local craftsmen

23 *Right* Members of the Watts family had been basket makers in Chipping Norton since the 1840s. Alfred Watts's shop was in Market Street from about 1887 to 1899. The geography of the street, where the pavement is much lower than the roadway, has obliged the photographer to place some of the family on boxes, so that their faces are not obscured by the railing

22 *Above* The sheep market in Chipping Norton about 1910. The fortunes of many such Cotswold towns were founded on wool. Morrison's cycle agency was opened in Middle Row in the 1890s. By 1910 the addition of 'motor' to his shop sign and his advertisement for petrol give an indication of changes on the way

24   *Above* High Street, Witney, 1890. The last building on
the right-hand side of the street is the Blanket Hall, built
soon after 1710 when the town's blanket-weavers were
incorporated by royal charter

25   *Below* Witney Market Place, 1900. At this time the
proprietor of the Temperance Hotel advertised 'Every
Accommodation for Commercial Gentlemen, Cyclists,
Tourists etc. Good Stabling. Covered Yard for Motors'

26 *Above* The Market Place at Witney, July 1900, with Church Green beyond. The Butter Cross in the foreground was built in the seventeenth century. By the time Henry Taunt took this photograph, it was probably no longer used for the sale of butter, poultry and eggs

27 *Below* The shop of W. Brooks in Bridge Street, Witney, 'decorated' for the Christmas of 1910

28   The sheep market in the Upper High Street, Thame, 1897. The great width of the street and the large number of public houses in it testify to the importance of Thame's market

29 Leicester House in Northfield End, Henley, 1860 – one
of the 'spacious and well-built houses' which the directories
of the period praise

30 *Below* The Market Place, Henley, in the early 1850s. The old Town Hall, built in the classical style in 1790, was replaced by the present red-brick building in 1899–1900. Henley was justly proud of its 'wide and handsome' streets, 'well-paved and gas-lighted'. The cannon was the sign for the inn of that name

31 *Right* Hart Street, Henley, 1906 or 1907. The shop on the corner of Bell Street, with its 'to let' notice on the wall, was a stationers and booksellers

32 *Right* The last sheep and cattle market held in Sheep Street, Bicester, 29 April 1910. The goods in the foreground are from Ashmore's hardware shop. The crowd has gathered outside Paxton and Holiday the auctioneer's office, next to the Crown Hotel

33, 34 *Left and below left* Bampton annual fair, 1904,
which took place on 26 and 27 August. The primary business
was the sale of horses, but, as with most country fairs,
trading was combined with the fun of sideshows, roundabouts
and swings, which attracted people from all the neighbouring
villages

35 *Below* Banbury Market Place and stalls in about 1860.
No. 21, the shop of Charles Pettit, draper, had been, in the
previous decade, the more elaborate establishment of
Prescott and Bloxham 'linen and woollen drapers, silk
mercers, hatters and carpet and rug warehousemen'

36 *Above* Church Street, Charlbury, in 1890. All activity in the street has come to a stop, so that the photographer, Henry Taunt, can take his picture

37 Banbury Market Place, 1907. The central building, then the shops of Hills and Rowney, picture-frame makers, and Miss A.E. Spencer, draper, had housed the Wool Hall, the Blue Coat School and the town gaol in previous centuries

38 *Left* Turrill's shop and delivery cart in Woodstock High Street, in about 1890, shortly after William Banbury Turrill had started business as a grocer and seedsman

VILLAGE LIFE

39   Wardington church path, August 1898

40   *Right* The main street in Souldern on a postcard of 1906.
As in many villages in Oxfordshire, the population of
Souldern decreased in the second half of the nineteenth
century. Although the inhabitants numbered only about 400
in 1906, the village still had two schools and a sub-post
office, two carpenters, a builder, a saddler, a blacksmith and
a boot maker, a grocer, two bakers, a coal merchant, a miller
and a public house, as well as seven farmers

41 *Above* Milcombe in about 1910. A typical scene in a
north Oxfordshire village

42 *Above* Harvest Festival at Langford Methodist Chapel in about 1900, with the music provided by harmonium and 'cello

43 *Left* Children on the green at Alvescot, in about 1910, with their parochial school and village pump in the background

Opposite page Three photographs from Filkins, in the west of the county, near the River Thames, show different forms of relaxation in a Cotswold village in the early years of this century

44 *Right* Tea on the lawn, c.1905

45 A peaceful smoke at the pub, *c.*1900

46 Old age in repose – Mrs Clapton in 1900

47 *Below* The blanket mill of William Smith and Co. at Crawley by the River Windrush in 1894. The blankets are stretched out on tenters in the sunshine, after hanging in sulphur fumes in the bleaching house

48 *Right* This post mill was built at Charlton on Otmoor in the seventeenth century and demolished in January 1905. Windmills were a common sight in the Oxfordshire landscape, until steam and electricity provided cheaper and more efficient methods of grinding corn

49 *Below* The family of the wheelwright and carpenter at Adderbury, 1904. At the feet of the older child is a beautiful toy horse and cart

50 *Right* The cider press of Edwin Gardner of Shilton, in about 1900. The press was taken round the villages of the area and people brought their own apples to be pulped in it

51 *Right* The interior of the blacksmith's cottage, Bampton, 1904. It is interesting to see the kettle on the range, the church almanack on the wall, and the smoked ham behind Mr Gibbard's right shoulder

52 *Left* Dorchester abbey and tollgate in about 1910. The pony and trap was taken by the photographer from another picture and added to this one in order to enliven the scene. This is why its wheels do not appear to rest on the ground

53 *Below* A party at the Golden Balls pub, 18 May 1888; at Standlake – a village in the west of the county

54 *Above* Standlake village cricket team in about 1895

61 *Above* The Saloon, Kirtlington Park, in about 1906. The handsome Palladian house was the home of the Dashwood family until 1909

62 *Below* The Great Hall of Broughton Castle at the beginning of this century, with fine examples of furnishing fabrics of the Shutford plush industry. The fourteenth-century castle, the seat of Lord Saye and Sele, was let to various tenants during the period, and once again became the family's residence in 1912

63   The Burford horse bus outside the Bull Hotel, 1889. Its
proprietor, Thomas Paintin, ran daily services from his office
in Sheep Street to Shipton railway station and to Witney
until about 1910. He also ran, first a grocery business, and
then a temperance hotel

64 The family of George Eaves, rope maker, with their pony
and trap at Williamscot, about 1890

65 *Above* Bicester's postman, Harry Hornsby, on his rounds, about 1900

66 *Above, right* Mrs Eliza Telford Simpson of The Temple, Goring, going visiting with her niece, Mrs Burnard, about 1902

67 *Right* The same Mrs Telford Simpson with Mrs Mary Aird at the wheel of a Ford passenger car, July 1903

68 Employees of Hook Norton Brewery, 1905, with the engine that had been bought the previous year

69 *Below* A Fowler traction engine, 'Victory', leaving Henley in a cloud of steam, on its way to tow guns in the Boer War, 1900

70 *Above* Traction engine on the Church Green, Witney, 1896, pulling the new boiler supplied by Daniel Young, engineer, to Charles Early's blanket mill

71 *Below* Steam barge of William Ward and Co., coal, coke and slate merchants, on the canal in Oxford in the 1890s

72 A Great Western train approaching Oxford from the north, in about 1883, in a photograph described by Henry Minn as one of the earliest instantaneous pictures taken in Oxford

73 *Above* The 'Fair Rosamund', a '517' class 0−4−2 T locomotive built in 1883, worked on the Woodstock branch line from its official opening in May 1890 to 1935. The man with his hand on the cab rail is the driver, Bob Pomeroy

74 *Below* A passenger train at Banbury's Great Western station in the 1890s. The coming of the railway in 1850 greatly improved Banbury's position as a market for the surrounding area. The London and North Western Railway opened in May and the G.W.R. in September of that year

75 Railway travel in the 1890s. Passengers watch anxiously
as their luggage is loaded at Banbury station

AT WORK

76   A shepherd with his sheep at Horspath, 1912

77 *Right* Ploughing with oxen in the Cotswolds, in about 1900. During the middle years of the nineteenth century this was a common sight in the county, but by 1900 they had been almost entirely replaced by horses and steam engines

78 *Above* Haymaking in the Henley area in about 1910

79 *Left* Reaping, *c*.1900. The use of the sail reaper considerably speeded up the cutting of the crop, but much manual labour was still needed to bind the sheaves

81 *Below* A wet plate photograph of the workers at John Moss's agricultural machine makers, Northfield End, Henley, 1850. For a while, John, who first appeared as a machine maker and millwright in Henley in 1830, was also a beer retailer, hence the advertisement for Clarkson's real beer

80 *Left* The Wyatt family of Hethe near Bicester with their horse-drawn reaper-binder at harvest time, in about 1900. Hornsby's machines, made in Britain from the 1880s, automatically tied the corn into bundles

82 *Below* Henry Glenister of the firm of Longs, wheelwrights, of Aston in Bampton, painting a wagon in about 1913. Members of the Long family had been wheelwrights in Aston and Cote from the early 1840s

83 *Right* A steam navvy at work in Ardley cutting in about 1908, on the line between Ashendon junction and Aynho junction. This short cut reduced the distance of the Great Western Railway's line between London and Birmingham by 8½ miles and was opened in 1910

84 *Below* Workmen repairing the Wheatley tunnel on the Oxford–Princes Risborough line of the Great Western Railway in 1883

85 Tying bundles of osiers at Jacob Beesley's yard north of Hythe Bridge in Oxford, 1901. Osiers were used to make eel-traps and all kinds of baskets

86 *Below* A wet plate photograph, taken in about 1850, of Henley's postman

87 *Left* The Boddington family, wheelwrights, established at Weston on the Green in 1883, with a circular saw powered by a small diesel engine, 1911

88 *Below, left* A group of workmen gathered for the laying of the foundation stone of the new Town Hall in Henley. It was built in 1899–1900, in red brick with stone facings, to commemorate Queen Victoria's Diamond Jubilee, and replaced the building seen in photograph no. 30

89 *Below* Boat building at Samuel Edgar Saunders's yard in Goring on Thames in about 1900. Advertisements of 1891 claimed that his patent boat fittings were the best in the trade. By 1907, he had sold boats to the King, the Admiralty, Trinity House and many yacht clubs

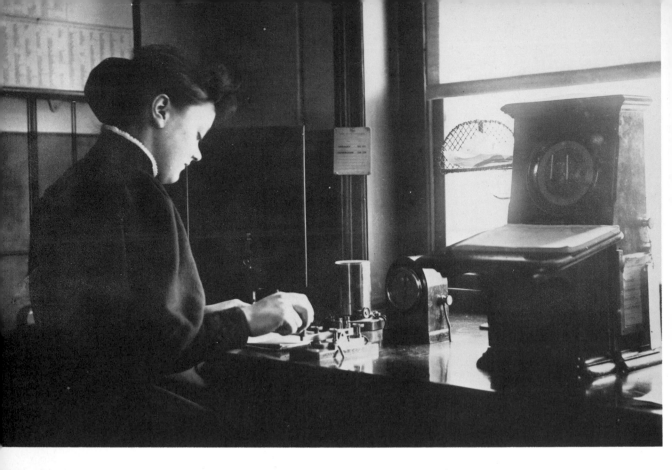

90 *Above* A new telegraph machine in operation in Banbury in the 1890s

91 *Left* Joe Alcock, plush-weaver, at his home in Sibford, in about 1900. He was employed by the firm of Wrench's of Shutford, which since 1815 had been manufacturing the velvet-like material for use in furnishing and clothes, especially servants' liveries and huntsmen's coats. An example of its use in furnishing can be seen in the photograph of the interior of Broughton Castle, not far from Shutford (no. 62)

Witney, on the banks of the River Windrush and on the edge of the Cotswolds has long been a centre of blanket making. Continuously from 1669 members of the Early family have been involved in the trade. The two photographs on the opposite page are from a series taken by Henry Taunt to illustrate a brochure of the firm, published in 1894

92 *Above* The loom shed in Early's blanket mill

93 *Below* Over-stitching the finished blankets. Coloured blankets were made for export only, mainly to South America

94 Bliss's tweed mill at Chipping Norton is well known to students of industrial architecture as a fine piece of Victorian factory building. During the winter of 1913–14, 280 workers at the mill went on strike when three members of their union were dismissed. The police had to guard the mill and the 130 non-unionists who continued working

96, 97 Compositors and office staff of the Church Army
Press, February 1904. This small printing works had opened
in the previous November in a disused chapel in Temple
Road, Cowley

98   The Weedon family playing croquet on the lawn of their house, The Temple, at Goring in about 1860

99 *Left* Mr and Mrs Arthur Telford Simpson with their great niece Monica Burnard in the grounds of their house by the Thames at Goring. They bought 'The Temple' in about 1897 and greatly altered it

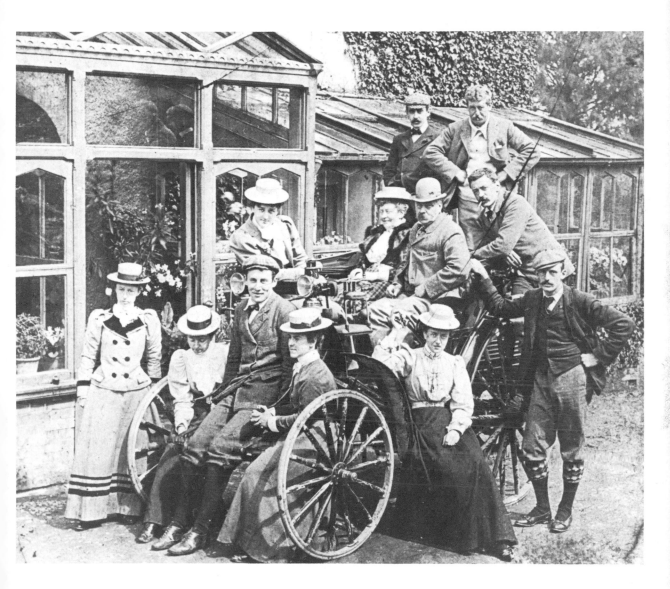

100 *Left* Tea on the lawn with the Telford Simpsons, about 1904. Mr Telford Simpson, chairman of several engineering firms, was a magistrate from 1899 and came to be known in Goring as 'Squire' Simpson as a result of his work and concern for the local community

101 *Above* A family outing at Yew Tree Farm, Brighthampton, about 1910

102 *Below* The setting up of the fair at Witney, September 1904. Behind the traditional swingboats and roundabouts can be seen Taylor's New Century Cinematograph

103 *Right* A closer view of Taylor's Cinematograph at the same fair. His carnival electric pictures are billed as 'bang up to date' and the illustrations of Boer War scenes proved extremely popular

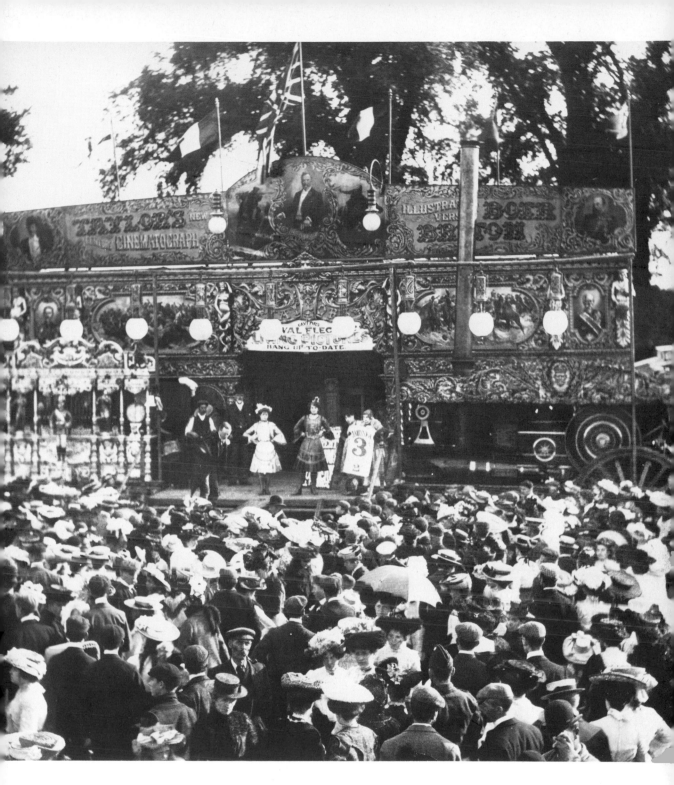

104 St Giles' Fair, Oxford, September 1904. Charles Thurston's 'colormatography' show had the added attraction of a mechanical organ by the famous Paris manufacturer, Marenghi. *Jackson's Oxford Journal* was very impressed with the large number of 'high class shows' that year, and with the extravagant use of electricity in arc and incandescent lights, which made the central avenue 'a most fascinating spectacle' after dark

105 *Above* The Bampton Morris Men in about 1890. Bampton is still one of the great centres of Morris dancing in this part of the country

106 *Above, right* Banbury Bowling Club in the 1890s. Bowling had long been a popular sport in the town, where the Old Central Club celebrated its tercentenary in 1884

107 *Right* The Rev. Arthur Majendie and the Woodstock orchestra in the late 1880s. The double bass and trumpet players are Messrs G. and J.G. Budd, the bakers

109 *Below* The Warwick hunt meets at Wroxton Abbey, the home of Lord North, about 1910

108 *Left* The meet of the Bicester hunt on Market Hill, Bicester, 1851. The hunt was established in about 1820. Its regular meets brought much trade to the town's inns and shops

110 *Below* Crowds gather to watch the hunt at Banbury Cross in about 1912

111 Playing fives at Bloxham School, 1882. Bloxham School was founded in 1853 as a Church of England boarding school for the sons of 'the professional classes', and much expanded in the 1860s

112 Bloxham School camera club, with three masters, J.H.T. Goodwin, E. Manley and W.J. Bridges, photographed in about 1880

113 *Left* Parents and teachers at a concert in Bloxham School grounds, 1890

114 *Right* Miss Edith Wood and her assistant in Chadlington infants' school, 24 July 1906, surrounded by their teaching aids

115 *Below* The 25 children who attended Waterstock's elementary school were all taught in the one room. For this photograph, taken on 16 March 1906, the boys were kept strictly separate from the girls

THE RIVER

121   Shiplake lock and mill, 1868. The first pound lock at
Shiplake was constructed in 1773, when the toll for barges
going through it was 1d per ton. It was entirely rebuilt in
1874. The mill, already in a ruinous condition, was
demolished in about 1907, as no tenant could be found

122 *Below* A fisherman with his nets and eel traps on the River Cherwell, photographed by Philip H. Delamotte, F.S.A., in 1857

123 *Right* Mr and Mrs Burnard and their daughter Monica on the landing stage of 'The Temple', Goring, in about 1904. In the boat are Mrs Telford Simpson and Mrs Schofield

124 *Right* The Telford Simpsons' steam launch 'Hera', ready for Henley Regatta, 1904. Mr Telford Simpson was a keen river man, a Thames Conservator and commodore of the Thames Sailing Club

127 *Above* H.W. Greene (seated), of Magdalen College, Oxford, with Colonel and Mrs Lindsay and Miss C. Bloomfield at Henley Regatta, 20 June 1892. The fashionable spectators were as much a part of the regatta as the skilled oarsmen

126 *Left* The regatta at Henley on Thames has long been Oxfordshire's most famous sporting event. Founded in 1839, it soon claimed first place among amateur rowing contests in England, and attracted competitors from all over the world. This photograph shows the final of the Thames Challenge Cup between Kingston and the Royal School of Mines in 1897

128 *Left* The Yale crew at Henley in the 1890s

129 *Below, left* The graceful eighteenth-century bridge over the Thames at Henley, with the tollgate, in the 1870s

130 *Below* Flooding in New Street, Henley, on 16 November 1894

132   An ingenious ice-yacht on the frozen Thames near
Henley during the winter of 1894–5

133 Boating in style at Goring for S.E. Saunders, the owner of the boat-building business there (see no. 89), in the late 1890s

134   Samuel Wilberforce (1805–1873), for nearly 25 years
Bishop of Oxford, called by some 'the greatest prelate of his
age' and by others 'Soapy Sam'. He transformed the
organization of the church in Oxfordshire

136 *Above* Samuel Wilberforce (centre, front row) and the archdeacon and rural deans of Oxfordshire, with whose help he revitalized church life and education in the county, 19 April 1866

137 *Left* William Morris, designer, poet and socialist, *c.*1890. He was associated with Oxfordshire through his purchase of Kelmscott Manor House on the banks of the Thames. He was active in attempts to preserve the county's old buildings, campaigning against changes like the restoration of Burford church in the 1870s and the widening of Magdalen Bridge in 1890

138 The Banbury Volunteers in the High Street in the early 1890s

139 *Left* The Woodstock troop of the Queen's Own
Oxfordshire Hussars on parade in St Giles, Oxford, 1897

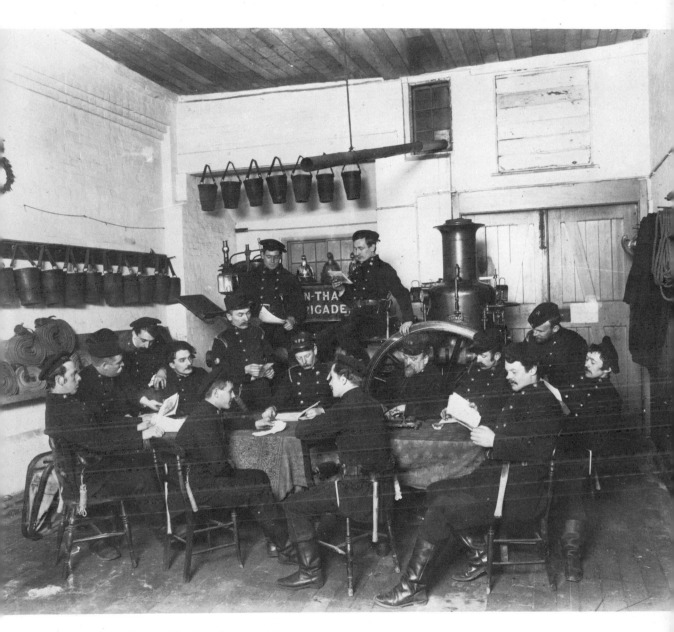

141 *Above* Henley Volunteer Fire Brigade in an elaborate
pose for the camera. Their equipment comprised one steam
engine, hose reels and buckets, and a fire escape, which can
be seen to the left of the table

140 *Left* The Mayor of Henley with the men of the town
who returned from the Boer War, 1902

142   Rally of fire brigades in Blenheim Park, 1898

143 A fine example of a trade union banner at a gathering of the United Kingdom Society of Coachmakers at Witney in about 1912

144 *Right* The tables laid for a celebration feast in Banbury for the Queen's Diamond Jubilee, 22 June 1897. A full day of entertainment marked the event in the town. It began with a 'feu de joie', a thanksgiving service, a procession and the starting of a new clock and chimes in the parish church in the morning. There were athletic sports and a military display in the afternoon. An illuminated fête in South Bar, Horse Fair and North Bar in the evening culminated in the lighting of a bonfire on Crouch Hill at 10 o'clock

145 *Below* A superb celebration tea for the children of Henley to mark the coronation of George V in 1911

146 In Bicester the Diamond Jubilee of 1897 was signalled by the firing of volleys on anvils in Market Square. Gunpowder on the anvil was touched off by the blacksmith with a red-hot hammer

147   The end of an era. Chipping Norton territorials going
off to the Great War in August 1914